Self-Therapy
Made Easy

Self-Therapy
Made Easy

Marian Van Eyk McCain

PSYCHE
BOOKS

Winchester, UK
Washington, USA

First published by Psyche Books, 2012
Psyche Books is an imprint of John Hunt Publishing Ltd., Laurel House, Station Approach,
Alresford, Hants, SO24 9JH, UK
office1@jhpbooks.net
www.johnhuntpublishing.com
www.psyche-books.com

For distributor details and how to order please visit the 'Ordering' section on our website.

Design: Stuart Davies

Printed and bound in the USA by Edwards Brothers Malloy

We operate a distinctive and ethical publishing philosophy in all
areas of our business, from our global network of authors to
production and worldwide distribution.

CONTENTS

Other books by Marian Van Eyk McCain

Transformation through Menopause
Elderwoman: Reap the wisdom, feel the power, embrace the joy
The Lilypad List: 7 steps to the simple life
GreenSpirit: Path to a New Consciousness (*as Editor*)
Downshifting Made Easy: How to plan for your planet-friendly future

Fiction

Apricot Harvest
The Bird Menders

To all those people who, over half a century, have shared with me their stories and their journeys, thank you. We have been teachers to each other.

Introduction

One of the most famous pieces of graffiti in the world was written on a wall in Delphi, in ancient Greece. It said 'γνῶθι σεαυτόν,' which means 'know thyself.'

These days, most of us know ourselves fairly well. We have had our astrological charts done, maybe even our palms read. We know not only our blood type but also our personality type—night owl/skylark, introvert/extravert, outgoing/reserved and so on. We have had our IQs tested—or tested them ourselves—and some of us have even been subjected to the MMPI, short for Minnesota Multiphasic Personality Inventory — a test designed to tell prospective employers absolutely everything they might want to know about your suitability for the job, plus a lot of other things that are none of their business anyway.

Not only have we measured ourselves in a number of these well-known ways, some of us are so addicted to measuring ourselves that we cannot resist even the silliest of quizzes in any magazine we come across. Have you ever thought a quiz was so daft that you were ashamed to answer it but you did it anyway, while no-one was looking, scribbling your scores on the back of an envelope and hastily throwing it away? (Yes, I am a closet quiz-taker too.)

Dale Carnegie's *How to Win Friends and Influence People*, the world's first 15 million copy self-help best-seller, was published in 1936. That was the year I was born. It also marks the beginning of what I call The Age of Pop Psychology. The fashions have changed, of course, as fashions do. Psychoanalysis is too slow and tedious for today's hurried culture. Transactional Analysis and Gestalt therapy, popular in the 1970s and brilliant for understanding our everyday behavior and the way we relate to others have given way to cognitive behavioral therapy in the popularity stakes. However, Neuro-Linguistic Programming, a methodology that also dates from the 1970s, is still alive and well, having been seized upon by corporate managers, salespeople, police and others with a vested interest in 'reading' the secrets of people's minds in the telltale micro-movements of their eyes or the patterns of their speech.

But regardless of trends, this Age is defined by the fact that many people alive today share an awareness of their inner lives and a facility for self-analysis which our ancestors did not have. We speak psychobabble as a second language. We know whether we come from Mars or Venus and how to communicate in 'I' messages, how to cut the ties that bind, how to say no without feeling guilty and how to love—or not to love—too much. We have come out of closets in droves with our sexuality and we have created a multi-million dollar industry out of personal growth and mind-body-spirit books. We have soaked up kitchen table wisdom and helped ourselves liberally to psychological chicken soup.

So of all the people who ever lived, we should be the best-adjusted, calmest, sanest, most sensible and enlightened lot you could ever hope to find. But on the basis that there is always room for one more book, what I am offering here aims to be the simplest, leanest and most effective of all primers for getting to know the really important things about yourself, dealing with the parts which are problematical and staying on course in your spiritual journey. It comes from a blend of my personal experience, my academic and clinical training and my many years as a workshop leader and transpersonal psychotherapist.

Part One is about self-knowledge and is a prerequisite for Part Two which explains the techniques of self-therapy. So this is a book intended to be read—for the first time anyway—in the order in which it is written, rather than dipped into randomly.

I could have expanded it into a huge book by explaining each concept in several different ways and including more case examples but I chose to keep it short and highly concentrated instead. Therefore to get the most out of it you will probably need to read it slowly and do some pondering between paragraphs.

Part I

THE MUSIC OF THE MIND:

Understanding your inner world

I

Playing Together

We are not soloists

The mind—what is it? Even to try and answer that question involves some sort of gymnastic feat because in order to examine the mind what can we use but...the mind?

We normally think about our minds in terms of the thoughts, ideas, feelings etc. that we are currently experiencing ("I had it in mind to..." "It crossed my mind that..." "What's on your mind?") as though it were a sort of TV set with some program or other currently playing. In a way, it is. However, it often feels as though somebody else is holding the remote. Thoughts, feelings and moods arise unbidden and often unwelcome. Programs play that are not of our choosing. Old movies come on that we would rather not watch. And efforts to switch off can sometimes be in vain. So what is going on?

Humans have been pondering that question since at least the 4th century BC and pretty much every model that anyone has come up with for understanding the way people think and feel and behave involves visualizing us as being composed of distinctly different selves. It is as though each of us, rather than being just one person, is actually several people rolled into one.

Plato, for example, saw every person as being animated by a soul that comprised three parts: the 'appetitive' part that governed basic things like survival, hunger, thirst, sex and so on, the 'rational' part that decides what's what, what's right or wrong and how we should live and the 'spirited' part that oversees it all and governs the emotions such as love and anger.

Duets: The conscious and unconscious mind

The key insight that laid the basis for much of modern psychology came from the work of Sigmund Freud in the late 19th century. Freud had similar ideas about those three aspects that rule the human, refining them into the instinct-driven Id, the parental, bossy Superego and the rational, decision-making Ego. However, he also saw the mind itself in terms of three divisions: the conscious (whatever is playing on the 'screen' right now), the pre-conscious (all the other things that *could* be playing on the screen if we clicked to change channels) and the unconscious (all the stuff that goes on behind the scenes but which we only ever catch glimpses of). And it is that third division that I want to concentrate on here for a moment.

First, let's collapse conscious and pre-conscious. Right now, you are probably thinking about what you are reading, so my words are front and center on your mental screen. Your tummy or bladder may also be suggesting that you put the book down and attend to their needs (most of us have more than one screen switched on, and although we can only attend to one of them at a time, we are aware of the others flickering). But what color is your front door? Do you have a cousin? How is your left foot feeling right now? Have you ever seen a flamingo?

Did you notice how easily the answers to those four questions came floating out of your pre-conscious as soon as I asked them? That is why, for the purposes of this discussion, I am treating the conscious and pre-conscious as one. The pre-conscious is merely the vast mental cupboard in which are stored all the things that you might potentially be thinking about, things you can easily bring on to your central screen just by thinking about them, much as you would take a spoon out of the drawer in your kitchen or a book off your shelf.

The unconscious, however, is a very different matter. Because what is stored in there will *not* come floating out easily on request. That is why it is called the *un*conscious.

The material is in there alright, but it cannot be brought out directly. We have to use various tricks and mirrors, clues and guesses in order to winkle it out.

So you might be asking: why do we need to winkle it out? Well, the biggest reason is that even though we are, by definition, unaware of everything hidden in our unconscious minds, it is the unconscious mind that dictates a lot of what we feel, and think, the ways in which we react to others and how we behave in our day to day life. You could almost think of the unconscious mind as a puppet master, hiding in the shadows and pulling our strings. The unconscious mind has a hand in choosing our careers, our homes, our friends and even our life partners. It influences pretty much everything we think and say and do and feel. So it is probably a good idea to get more familiar with its contents.

Not all therapists are interested in their clients' unconscious minds. The pure behaviorists, for example, have been trained to see the mind as a 'black box' and ignore what goes on inside it. Just as a computer technician these days would deal with a problem in your laptop by simply replacing the motherboard (and neither they nor you would ever know what the problem had been) the goal of the behavioral therapist is purely to replace dysfunctional behavior with something more functional. He or she is less interested in understanding you than in retraining you to behave differently. This method usually works just fine for dogs and horses, and parents use it successfully with their children much of the time. For some situations and some problems, it works with adults. In fact we use a similar technique on ourselves whenever we make an effort to replace what we see as a 'bad habit' with a better alternative, without necessarily knowing—or caring—why we developed the bad habit in the first place. This is great if it works, and sometimes it does.

What frequently happens, though, is that we succeed for a while and then we lapse. Then we beat ourselves up for failing. We try again. We manage it for a while and then once again we lapse, which of course makes us even more cross with ourselves. (Does this pattern sound familiar?)

However, if we consider the role of the unconscious mind, this should not surprise us at all. Whenever we try to change our own behavior and find ourselves sabotaged, it is highly likely that the saboteur lurks in our own unconscious mind.

There are many kinds of therapy, therefore, that aim to reveal the contents of the unconscious mind. Since knowledge is power, the more we know about this aspect of ourselves, the better we understand our motives, vulnerabilities and fears, the more empowered we feel and the better able we are to deal with issues, change dysfunctional behavior and relate to others. The unmasked saboteur becomes immediately easier to outwit. Even if we never succeed in outwitting him or her completely, at least we can act much more swiftly and limit the damage to a very great extent. So all the techniques and exercises you will find in this book are drawn from this latter type of therapy. I have cherry-picked the ones that have proved most useful and effective, both in my clinical practice and in my own journey of self-awareness.

Trios: The Observing Self

I started this chapter by remarking that in order to examine the mind we have no choice but to use...the mind! This brings us to a very important concept in self-therapy. It is the cornerstone of self-therapy, so we need to address it early in the process. This is the concept of the Observing Self.

The Observing Self is a third level of mind which we can deliberately cultivate in order to observe in a totally neutral way—i.e. without blame, judgment or interference—our behavior, our thoughts, our feelings and moods and all the workings of our own minds. Even though total objectivity is impossible for the human mind to achieve, developing a strong and capable Observing Self is probably the closest we can ever get to it. For the purposes of self-therapy, it is the best we can do, and it is probably good enough. It should be added here that the Observing Self operates *in addition to and at the same time as* both the conscious and the unconscious minds, rather than as a replacement for either of them. It is like a CCTV camera that we switch on, its only role being to observe and record but never to interfere.

Quartets: The Collective Unconscious

Carl Jung (1875-1961), who as well as being a clinician and researcher did an enormous amount of self-observation and self-therapy, discovered evidence of yet another, deeper layer of mind that he termed the 'collective unconscious.' This, unlike the personal unconscious, is a layer of being that we share with the rest of our species and probably with other species of animals also. In Jung's own words, it is a:

> "...psychic system of a collective, universal, and impersonal nature which is identical in all individuals. This collective unconscious does not develop individually but is inherited. It consists of pre-existent forms, the archetypes, which can only become conscious secondarily and which give definite form to certain psychic contents."

If you have ever tried to rid your garden of couch grass, you will have discovered that each individual grass blade (conscious mind) has deep roots going every which way (unconscious mind) and way below that is what feels like a vast and even deeper system of roots that seems to go down into the bowels of the Earth and to cover the whole garden (collective unconscious).

For example, many of the typical feelings and behavior patterns that come with being male or female — the Mars and Venus characteristics — arise from this collective, instinctual place, regardless of who we are as individuals, and it is important to acknowledge their origins.

Jung is also famous for his model of the mind that describes four key functions — thinking, feeling, intuition and sensation — each of which is developed to a greater or lesser extent in each individual. The goal of Jungian-based therapy is what Jung called 'individuation,' i.e. becoming as complete and fully ourselves as we can possibly be by developing all four functions to the best of our ability and integrating the various parts of ourselves into a healthy whole.

Quintets and ensembles: Our inner 'family'

In the early 1970s there was a very popular model for understanding the human mind and behavior called Transactional Analysis.[1] Developed by Eric Berne (1910-1970), this captured the public imagination when Berne published his best-selling book *Games People Play* in 1965. The book looked at the way we structure time (e.g. intimacy, rituals, pastimes and games) and gave cute names to the most common games, such as NIGYSOB ('Now I've got you, you son of a bitch,') 'Wooden leg,' 'Schlemiel,' 'Let's you and him fight,' the ever-popular 'Why don't you?...Yes, but...' and many more.

Even though Transactional Analysis (or TA for short) is less fashionable nowadays as a therapeutic tool, many of Berne's concepts and the catchy terms he coined have passed into our everyday conversation, such as the idea that people trade with each other in a currency of 'strokes' (units of recognition) ranging from the smallest nod to everyone's favorite type of stroke, the 'warm fuzzy' and everyone's least favorite, the 'cold prickly.'

One of the most useful of Berne's ideas was the one known as 'Structural Analysis' or the 'PAC model.' This is the idea that every one of us, rather than being a singular person, is actually five people rolled into one—a Parent (subdivided into the Nurturing Parent and the Critical Parent), an Adult and a Child (the latter also subdivided and comprising the Natural Child and the Adapted Child).

At any given moment, one of these five 'ego states' is being expressed. When we are seeking or exchanging information, dealing in facts, solving a crossword or a Sudoku puzzle, tracing our route on a map or doing anything else that requires a lot of thinking and rationality but virtually no feeling or emotion, the Adult ego state is operating.

When we are judging or criticizing someone or something, when we are being bossy, condescending or patronizing or when we find ourselves lecturing somebody who has displeased us in some way (including ourselves), then the Critical Parent ego state has taken over. This applies even if we are only *feeling* judgmental or *imagining* ourselves giving someone a telling-off.

In those moments, however, when we reach out to another with kindness or compassion, think a kindly thought, do something nice for somebody, comfort a sobbing child or listen sympathetically to a friend's problem, our ego state has switched to Nurturing Parent.

The Natural Child ego state is probably everyone's favorite ego state. It is your Natural Child who enjoys chocolate, who loves to walk barefoot on the beach, soak in a warm bath, cuddle, dance and sing. ("The Kid in me" is yet another example of the way Berne's ideas have woven themselves into our everyday language.)

But the kid within us has another side: the one we call the Adapted Child. Just as a young tree growing in a forest will bend and twist as it moves upwards in its constant search for the light, the human child will bend and twist in a constant search for affection, attention and appreciation. Thus the adult forms of both tree and child retain, to a large extent, the shape of their youth. Each child, in adapting to the familial and cultural environment into which he or she is born, develops a set of learned responses and behaviors which persist into adulthood. Most of them, such as 'good manners,' are useful and benign and in fact essential for living as a responsible member of society. Some are not. As children, our innate need to survive leads us to develop whatever strategies seem to work in our particular circumstances and these strategies will obviously vary according to our personalities and circumstances. So the child of an abusive parent may find that the best strategy is to run and hide, whereas another child in a similar situation may learn to lie, a third may learn that the best defense is to go on the attack and another discovers that the safest thing is to grovel and try to please.

It is amazing and wonderful that children are so resilient and adaptive that they can survive—and even thrive—in even the most dreadful circumstances. But this survival has a cost. The cost is that when we grow up and are no longer dependent on our parents and families for our survival, we find that our unconscious minds have retained all those childhood strategies, just as a dog you adopted from the rescue center might still exhibit signs of old patterning from its former life. The Adapted Child lives on within us and we find ourselves running away, hiding, lying, attacking, groveling, placating etc. even though our conscious minds know perfectly well that in a marriage, in the workplace or with a good friend these very strategies that once ensured our survival have now become a hindrance.

Remember, it is not just people from dysfunctional families who develop childhood survival strategies: we *all* do. Every child makes individual adaptations to the family it is part of, just as every puppy does. Whatever behavior earned us most recognition and attention in childhood, whether positive or negative, is likely to become a feature of our adulthood also. If getting good grades at school was what earned us the biggest chunks of praise and recognition from our parents, we shall probably go on being achievers all our lives, in order to please our internalized 'parents.' If we got praised for our helpfulness, we have probably grown into helpful adults but if the only time anyone noticed us was when we did something outrageous, we may still be trying to shock the world into taking notice.

We shall speak again of childhood survival strategies. But for now, remember that this quintet of ego states, which straddle both the conscious and unconscious portions of the mind, always has the collective unconscious playing the bass line. And with any luck, the Observing Self will be there too—not playing: just listening.

The full orchestra

Before we leave this tour of the mind, there is one more way of looking at the mysteries of mind that I want to include. We have already looked at the distinctions between conscious, pre-conscious and unconscious, the way we switch between various ego states, the development of childhood survival strategies and how these can harden into adult character-istics. But the actual, lived *experience* of having a mind with all these different components to it is that sometimes it feels as though we are not just one person, or two or three or even five but in fact a whole cast of characters, any one or more of whom might be on stage at any given time. We might snap at our partners and then mutter, in remorse and bewilderment, "Where did *that* come from?" We hear a voice inside our heads berating us, criticizing us, putting us down, "You idiot! What did you do *that* for?" We find ourselves in inner struggles as though there were two sumo wrestlers battling for supremacy within our minds, one wanting to get the work done, the other wanting to check Facebook, or one yearning for a flat belly and the other yearning for an iced donut.

Roberto Assagioli (1888-1974) believed, like Carl Jung, that the goal of therapy should be integration of all the parts of the self and the integration of the individual self with the greater self, i.e. with both the collective unconscious and the transpersonal realm — the spiritual whole of which our immortal souls form a part. Thus his model is known as Psychosynthesis.

Assagioli did not believe in labeling certain behaviors as pathological. He regarded every human being as:

> "... *a fundamentally, healthy organism in which there may be temporary malfunctioning. Nature is always trying to re-establish harmony, and within the psyche the principle of synthesis is dominant. Irreconcilable opposites do not exist. The task of therapy is to aid the individual in transforming the personality, and integrating apparent contradictions."*

One of the techniques for doing that, which I think you will enjoy trying out (see Chapter 8) is to look more closely at your inner cast of characters — inner critics, sumo wrestlers, needy kids, bullying dads and all — and to get them talking to each other.

In this chapter, I have tried to give you a satellite map of the way human minds generally function. This is essential. You would naturally expect that any therapist you go to would have an understanding of such things, so if you are going to be your own therapist then you, too, must have this sort of background information. You must also have some diagnostic skills. It is one thing to know about human minds in general, but although we are essentially similar in our functioning each of us is unique. So you need to learn a few things about *your* mind in particular. That is where we are going next.

2

Learning the Score

Note: We are going to start this process where the therapist would start: by getting to know you, the individual. So please read these early chapters slowly and as you move through the various points take time to ponder on how each of them might apply in your own life. It could even be helpful to make notes as you go along.

Chords and melodies: background and foreground

Once you know a bit about how minds in general tend to work and start to look at your own mind, there are two important things you need to look at. We call them Nature and Nurture. A battle raged for many decades over which played the bigger role in the formation of a human being. Nowadays, it is generally agreed that the most important thing is neither Nature nor Nurture alone but how they interact in any given individual.

Many of our genes, the biologists are now saying, only *predispose* us to certain behaviors, certain illnesses and so on. The gene may or may not be expressed and we may or may not exhibit those behaviors or fall prey to those illnesses. Whether they are expressed or not often depends on our environment. A child with two highly musical parents who has inherited perfect pitch, if adopted into a family with no interest in music, may never play an instrument and may only ever sing in the shower: never at Carnegie Hall.

Psychologist James Hillman talks about the 'acorn' of interest within a child that may later become his or her life's work.[2] But the acorn can only germinate if it falls on the right soil and gets enough water to grow.

So let's first look at the background of your life. Not your genome, since we have no lab to do it in, but the basic background of who you are now, as an adult: your type, your personality etc.

The background

Your physical type is largely inherited, as is your geographical and cultural background, your family background and so on. All of those are 'givens.' Beyond that, as I suggested earlier, it is likely you have already classified yourself in one of the many ways that human beings have devised for sorting people into different types. The earlier ones, like the ancient Greek theory of the four 'humors' and the Indian Ayurvedic system of *doshas* based on five elements, all involved the physical aspects of self (e.g. body shape) as well as the mental. Astrology, of course, uses totally different criteria. Many modern typologies are based on answers to questionnaires. One of the latter that I find particularly useful is the Myers-Briggs typology which grew out of the work of Carl Jung.

Jung described four basic functions of the human mind: sensation, thinking, feeling and intuition. Although we use all four, there are very few of us who use them all equally. We all know people who are primarily 'thinking types.' Those we describe as 'good with their hands' are 'sensate types.' These two functions often go together and a 'thinking/ sensate' person is the ideal one to call on if you need help getting your kitchen remodeled. For most of us, one of the four functions will be primary, another will be secondary and the other two may lag further behind. Individuation is about bringing those lagging functions up to speed as we age and evolve.

Jung also divided us into introverts and extraverts. The test for this is not whether you like being with other people or not (most introverts also enjoy companionship) but by how you recharge. An introvert, stressed by being around others too long, yearns for quiet and solitude. An extravert, stressed by too much aloneness, seeks out company in order to recharge.

Another interesting way in which we vary in our preferences, according to Jung, is seen in our general approach to the world around us. Either we simply perceive something or we judge it. Naturally we all do both, depending on circumstances, but not at exactly the same time. The one we more habitually do is called a P preference or a J preference.

Mother and daughter duo Katharine Briggs and Isabel Myers together developed a system for combining Jung's functions and preferences into a table of sixteen types of people, with a comprehensive and thorough set of questions that can reliably classify an individual into one of the sixteen.[3]

The typologies mentioned here are only some of the many available. It is beyond the scope of this book to describe any more of them or to describe any of them in detail. Besides which, no description of a typology is any use without including the tools for determining where *you* fit. So you will find neither the descriptions of the various types nor the measurement tools here. However, they are readily available elsewhere, in libraries, in bookstores, in classes and workshops and all over the Internet and it can be extremely useful to look at yourself through all of these different lenses. It will build up, in layers, your understanding of who you are, how you are and why. Plus it may also shed some light on why your significant others are the way *they* are. That, in turn, can be enormously helpful in understanding and resolving any conflict that might occur in your relationships, at home, with friends or in the workplace.

After this brief look at the background of who you are, as an individual, let's look at what has been superimposed on it—and by what means. Following that, we can get into the most important part of the book: how to work with all this.

The foreground

Sara and the monkey

Many years ago, when Alex and Sara were backpacking around the world, they had a stormy argument right in the middle of a square in Athens because Alex—being the generous person he is—had given some of their food to another couple of backpackers. Naturally, it is fine to share food. But he had given them the bag of dried cherries that Sara specially liked and she was afraid they wouldn't be able to find any more that tasted as nice.

Not only did Sara feel ashamed of herself for being so petty—not to mention the embarrassment of arguing with her partner in public—but she also felt overcome with huge waves of guilt. It was such a small thing, and yet there she stood, in the middle of Athens, in tears, feeling like a very small child.

Whenever we find ourselves feeling little, it is a sure sign that something important from our childhood is being triggered. The question to ask—right there and then if you can—is "When have I felt like this before?"

That's what Sara asked herself, standing in the square that day. And the memory swam straight into her awareness, on cue. She is five years old. It is early December. The church is having a toy service and all the children are being asked to donate something. But not just an old toy they don't play with any more. "A true Christian," the vicar emphasizes, *"Gives something that he or she really values."* Sara has been intending to donate the farm set that she rarely plays with. (It is still brightly painted and looks new.) But now she is staring at Munko, her beloved toy monkey, with one eye missing and his stuffing starting to come out and she is thinking that she really should be donating him instead, because she values him much more than the farm set. She just can't do it though. She loves him too much. She is going to give them the farm set. What a wicked, un-Christian girl she is. Sara is flooded with guilt and so very ashamed of her selfishness.

It seems crazy now, to Sara's adult mind, to think that battered old Munko with his missing eye would have made a better gift for some other child than an as-new farm set. And yet, as this story so clearly demonstrates, our conscious, adult minds are being influenced all the time by things like this from our unconscious.

We saw earlier that some of the stuff in our unconscious minds is based on the survival strategies we developed in infancy and childhood. Those strategies actually grew right there in the unconscious, since most of them began before we were big enough to devise them consciously. Sara's story, however, shows that stuff can also get there *via the child's conscious mind*, i.e. when injunctions from an authority figure like a parent, a teacher—or in this case the vicar—become internalized as 'rules to live by.' Unless we review these with our adult mind we might go on following them for the rest of our lives without knowing it (or, like Sara with those dried cherries, feeling guilty when we 'break' them). If we don't review them as adults, we never realize how inappropriate many of them have now become. I always think of this review process as being akin to coming across some old object in the attic (or basement or garage or wherever you store things) and deciding whether or not you still have a use for it.

Some of our rules, fortunately, get reviewed automatically as we age. For example, following the rule 'Always give up your bus seat to an adult,' which was highly appropriate in my childhood, would be nonsensical now that I'm 76.

Although the messages we hear in our developmental years come originally from someone else, once they pass into our unconscious minds they change slightly and also become firmer and less flexible, just as a floppy lump of dough put in an oven turns into a solid loaf. We call this process 'introjection.' Through introjection, those outer voices become inner voices. The stern teacher, the angry parent or bossy older sibling shape-shift into the Inner Critic—the part of us that is always finding fault with the rest. Fortunately, for our purposes of revealing what is in our unconscious minds, they often leave a big clue, which is that the Inner Critic tends to talk in a very similar voice to that teacher, parent or sibling and to use the same sort of language. My own Inner Critic, if ever she chides me for getting in a rage about something, says "You mustn't lose your temper" exactly the way my mother used to say it when I was four years old.

Family traditions easily get absorbed into the unconscious mind, as do cultural traditions. We do things a certain way because 'that's the way it is supposed to be done.' And that, of course, is perfectly fine as long as we are comfortable with it. If it works, why fix it? But when doing things that way brings any kind of discomfort, that is a signal to look more deeply, for it may mean that some ancient, introjected rule needs excavating, examining and possibly revising.

The PAC model we looked at earlier is useful here. A parent takes a young child by the hand to cross the road because the parent knows how to cross roads. As the child grows, he or she is taught the rules for crossing roads and encouraged to practice. "Which way do we look first?" and so on. The child learns consciously how to cross roads but eventually he or she can cross a road without even thinking about it. The knowledge has passed from the outer parent to the inner Parent. The Parent part of our psyche plays the role of automatic pilot, freeing the Adult to concentrate on things that actually need figuring out. Imagine how laborious it would be if, every time you needed to cross a road, you had to figure out how best to do it, all over again. Anyone who has gone from the UK to the US or vice versa knows that from experience. (It is why so many intersections in London have 'look left' or 'look right' painted on the ground in large, white, unmissable letters, with arrows!)

When you consider how many things in our lives come as automatically to us as crossing roads, you can see how much we rely on our inner, Parent self to hold that vast database of knowledge and wisdom and use it to guide us through each day. The Parent is an invaluable part of our psyche. Just as our actual parent(s) looked after us in childhood, our own inner Parent self looks after us now. That is its role, to look out for us and make sure our best interests are served. Sometimes it does so in gentle and loving ways (The Nurturing Parent), sometimes it is neutral, as with crossing roads, and at other times it can be stern, strict and even harsh (the Critical Parent) but let us always remember that its basic intent—like that of any parent—is to take care of us. One of the most important bits of self-therapy we can do is to enlist its help in dealing with our issues and in making decisions.

While we are on the subject of background and foreground we need to look at how our family structures influence who we are, but since there is a chronology element in that, it forms part of the next chapter, which is all about our development over time.

3

The March of Time: Understanding your life story

We are shaped by our race, our place, our gender, our region, our religion, our culture, our families etc. Each of these main elements shapes us in both background ways and foreground ways. Take gender, for example. Although there is a surprisingly large chunk of middle ground which can cause considerable heartache for those who find themselves in it, most of us are born definitively male or female. That is background, fixed firmly in our DNA. Our particular culture's—and family's—attitude to sex roles is in the background also. In the foreground, however, is the set of expectations, beliefs and rules we personally absorb from that background about being male or female and how to express our sexuality. In other words, background is what we come into and foreground is what we make of it. What we make of it is what we become. Our personal process of becoming—our evolution as individuals, or as Jung would call it our individuation—starts at conception and continues until we die.

In this chapter, we look at that process as it develops over time. We have already touched on the early childhood part of it when we spoke of survival strategies. Let's look at some more of the things that shape us in our formative years.

Shaped by trauma

Learning about post-traumatic stress disorder in combat veterans reminds us that trauma can have long-lasting effects. Trauma early in our lives, when our personalities are still forming, can be even more devastating. Fears, anxieties, phobias and many other problematic things in our adult lives can be traced back to childhood traumas. And remember that an ordinary event—such as getting temporarily lost in a large department store—could easily constitute a trauma for a three-year old.

Shaped by stories

My top favorite story, when I was very small, was one of Rudyard Kipling's *Just So Stories* of how certain animals got to be the way they are. It was 'The Elephant's Child,' the tale of the—originally trunkless—young elephant who used to get into trouble with all his adult relatives because he was always asking questions. Determined to find out for himself the answer to his query about what crocodiles eat for dinner, he went on a long and adventurous journey, met a crocodile (who answered his question by pulling his nose so hard that it became hugely elongated), had more adventures on the way home and got his own back on those pesky relatives by beating the hell out of them with his new trunk.

My favorite book at age eight was about a bunch of little woodland creatures who lived together in a very co-operative community where everyone did whatever he or she was best at doing, everyone's needs were met and goods and services were exchanged without the use of money.

Some of my character traits, much of my subsequent life story and many of my interests can all be discerned in the early stories that I loved. In them, I can see my unquenchable curiosity about everything around me. I see my career as a therapist who was continually asking questions. I see my love of travel and adventure, of wildlife, and of scientific research. I see my youthful move into independent thought and my scorn for the ideas of family members who still thought they knew better than I did. I see my political beliefs, my philosophy of life and the importance of home, community and co-operation.

You might try thinking about which stories, books, movies etc. were your childhood favorites and what that can tell you about the adult you now are. You may be surprised.

Shaped by families

Some of the stories you heard in childhood may also have been family stories that get passed down for generations (my grandmother told tales of a wacky relative called Cousin Lizzie, famous for her escapades). But even without family stories, we usually take on some coloration from our families of origin. Or, if we disliked the way our families were, we deliberately did it differently once we were grown up. Was yours a family of readers? Of campers, hikers, birdwatchers, hard drinkers, gamblers, TV watchers? Was it a musical family? A sporty family? A religious family? Were they demonstrative or reserved? Did the family sit down to dinner together? How was conflict resolved?

When you look at yourself now, can you see which family patterns you took on and which you made a point of rejecting? Most of us end up doing a bit of both.

Our families shape us in other, less obvious ways. We talk a lot about parental influence on children but sibling influence is no less powerful. Parents think they know what goes on between siblings but much of it takes place way below the parental radar. If you have an older sibling who criticized or bossed you, your Inner Critic may well have the voice of that older brother or sister.

Birth order shapes us in other ways too. When I ran parenting classes I used to do an exercise that involved dividing the class into five groups based on family position: oldest child, youngest child, middle child, only child and 'parental child' (i.e. a child with very much younger siblings who had helped to look after them). As each group discussed how they felt, it soon became obvious that family position brings with it a bunch of typical feelings and reactions. Eldests often grumble that they had to fight for privileges and that their younger sibs 'had it easy.' Yet they often choose careers that involve taking charge or taking care of others. Youngests often have the hardest time breaking away because they are the last to leave the nest. Middles tend to feel ignored, overlooked, less important…and so on.

As well as positions based on birth order, families also have 'slots.' In small families, this is often not important, but in larger families it can be, especially for the younger children. Every child has a need to be special in some way. So if one child in the family shines at sport, one is academic and gets praised for good exam results, another is musical and a fourth one is artistic, by the time the fifth one comes along and finds those four slots already taken, it is harder to find a suitable one. So he or she might choose the 'rebel' slot in a desperate attempt to be recognized as different and thus worthy of attention. Hence the well-known phenomenon of the 'black sheep.' It is a tough role, but at least it gets lots of attention!

Shaped by life

For at least twenty-five centuries, people have been describing the human lifecycle as being divided into a series of stages. Starting at birth, we move from stage to stage, each stage having its own psycho-social tasks that need completing before we can move on to the next. Confucius divided it into six stages and Solon, in ancient Greece, described ten. In our own time, especially since Freud and Jung, there have been a number of other models developed. The eight-stage model described by Erik Erikson (1902-1994) is one of the best-known. In the first year and a half of life, Erikson said, a well cared for infant develops a basic sense of trust. An ill-treated or neglected infant is likely to grow up with a mistrust of the whole world—and to remain that way. Toddlerhood is when we develop a feeling of autonomy. Failure to do so may leave us with a lifelong sense of shame or guilt. During the pre-school years, we begin to assert power over our environment and that leads to the capacity for initiative and the ability to assume leadership when necessary. Our early school years, if we cope well with them, leave us with an inner sense of competence and self-assurance. Too many problems at this stage can result in feelings of inferiority. The task of adolescence is to gain a strong sense of one's own identity.

In young adulthood, our attention is focused on building and maintaining relationships. If this stage turns out badly it can result in a sense of isolation. It is during middle adulthood that we give our gifts to the world through our work and our creativity in whatever form it takes and by teaching and mentoring others. After retirement, we reap the harvest of our lives, moving into a time of wisdom and looking back on our lives with a sense of fulfillment rather than regret.

My favorite was devised much more recently by Bill Plotkin, whose model, twenty-five years in the making, is in the shape of a wheel, divided into eight stages. He calls it 'Eco-Soulcentric Development.'[4] It describes not only the eight major stages of healthy development that are grounded in interaction with Nature (within and without) but also the trajectory of the dysfunctional (egocentric) development that has become so common in today's materialistic society. According to Plotkin, some people never successfully complete the inner, psychological tasks of adolescence, which are not only the formation of a healthy identity—what Plotkin calls 'a secure and authentic social self'— that can function successfully in the world outside the family, but also the formation of a personal set of thought-through values that is not merely a replica of what is offered by a materialistic consumer culture.

Using a vivid set of double metaphors, Plotkin describes in rich detail the tasks, challenges and outcomes of each stage, the archetypal energies (from the collective unconscious) that govern each of them and the gifts that each stage enables us to offer to our communities and to the world in general. And like those others, from Confucius to Erikson, he includes useful advice for parents in guiding their children through the early stages. As you may imagine, one such piece of advice is about encouraging children to think for themselves and limiting their exposure to consumerism and particularly to TV.

The element Plotkin brings to his model that was absent from Erikson's is the ecological one. Our species, in cutting ourselves off from wild Nature, insulating ourselves in air-conditioned, centrally-heated buildings, watching the world on a screen instead of first-hand, is in danger of losing its age-old feelings of connectedness with the seasons, the natural cycles of Nature and its sense of belongingness—to the land, to the region, to family, tribe and community. This has created a vacuum in the human psyche—a spiritual vacuum which we try to fill with consumer goods, addictive substances, mindless entertainment and adrenalin-boosting activities. Sadly, it has made us less concerned about the mess we have been making of the planet.

All of us are, to a greater or lesser extent, shaped by these cultural trends. 21st century life, whilst more comfortable in many ways than that of previous centuries, is in many other ways more challenging. So an important part of self-therapy is taking a hard look at what effects your cultural environment is having on you. Many of the personal stresses that bring so many people into therapy are exacerbated by the huge level of what I call 'background stress' that affects everyone else as well.

Transitions

Our lives are studded with transitions of one kind or another. Being born is the first big one and dying is the last. In between, the passage from each stage to the next involves a period of transition. Some transitions are traditionally marked by a ritual, (though many of these, such as the Jewish bar mitzvah that marks puberty, are confined to certain religious or racial groups) but many are not. Unlike some older cultures which have retained their *rites de passage*, our modern, Western culture has very few and it is probably poorer for that since ritual can be enormously helpful in aiding the process of moving from stage to stage.

Transition of any kind follows a predictable pattern, with a beginning, middle and end. It begins with an ending. Toddlerhood ends on the first day of pre-school. Adolescence begins with the end of childhood. Moving house begins with saying goodbye to the old neighborhood. Retirement begins with the goodbye speeches in the office. A new journey begins with leaving the house, the train station, the shore — or the ground. This stage frequently involves loss and grieving. Many brides weep the night before their weddings. I cried when my youngest was weaned and I knew I would never again be able to experience the joy of breast-feeding. I cried when my kids started school and when my nest was empty. No true transition is without some degree of pain, however small. (That is why tribal puberty rites often involve ritual cutting — circumcision, facial cuts, tattoos etc.)

The middle part is often the hardest to get through. Often called the 'neutral zone,' it is an in-between sort of place where you are out of one reality but not yet into the next. There are often feelings of lostness, of not belonging anywhere, of marking time, waiting, wondering and sometimes of flip-flopping between realities. Teenagers who behave like kids one minute and adults the next are a good example of this.

This middle stage may last for hours, days, weeks, months or even years, but it always feels like a sort of no-person's land. It is a bit like one of those road or rail tunnels under the water, like the one under the English Channel or the one between downtown Boston and the airport, because once you are in it you can no longer see either the place you came from or the place you are going to and you have no choice but to stay down there out of the daylight and keep moving forward, hoping the roof will not collapse.

Then, one day, it is over. The transition is complete and it has ended with your shiny new beginning. The butterfly emerges from the cocoon, dries off, unfurls its wings and flies into a new future.

Some transitions are major ones that take us from stage to stage in our cycle of development. Baby becomes toddler, toddler becomes schoolboy, boy becomes man, man becomes elder: girl becomes maiden, maiden becomes mother (literally or figuratively) and mother becomes crone. Along the way there are dozens of smaller transitions: school to college, starting work, moving into and out of intimate relationships, marriage, parenthood, moving house, changing jobs, menarche and menopause, loss, illness, recovery/rehabilitation, bereavement, divorce, retirement...

Since the transitional periods of our lives can be challenging and difficult, these are often the times when we feel most keenly the need for expert help: someone to talk to, someone to assist us in navigating our way through stormy waters. Sometimes, transitions are so tricky that we become stuck in the neutral zone, unable to move. Therapy can be the board under our back wheels that gets us out of the mud.

Reframing

Therapy also teaches us to see familiar things differently. Therapists call this 'reframing': putting old pictures in new frames in order to see them in a fresh way. My first marriage ended in divorce. It felt like a failure at the time, but later, when I looked back at all the things it taught me about myself, I started seeing it as a learning experience. Every relationship we are in has lessons to teach. Every interaction we have with another is a potential mirror held up to ourselves. Every one of life's experiences is potentially a lesson and everyone you meet is both your teacher and your pupil. It is one long learning curve. One of my teachers used to say "There are no mistakes, only outcomes."

Diving in

There is little point in paying for therapy if you are not going to benefit from it. But to gain the benefit you have to dive into it. (It is like swimming. First you have to give yourself to the water, trust the water to hold you up.) When I was a therapist and a new person came to see me, after she had finished telling me about her problem and what she wanted to change I used to ask her to move to a different chair and tell me all the reasons why she *didn't* want to change and how she thought she might sabotage the therapy. We saved a lot of time that way. Because most people, when they go into therapy, also have a resistance to it. And with good reason: it can be painful! There are things we don't want to discover about ourselves.

I know someone who lost her husband in a mining accident and became, overnight, a grieving widow. That was nine years ago and she has been stuck in grieving widowhood ever since. The last time I saw her she told me how she had been to seven different therapists and they were all incompetent. I think she is afraid of coming undone. Yes, therapy *is* capable of bringing people undone and that can feel scary. It is also designed to help them reassemble the pieces in a new way, but the undoing has to happen first. So it is no wonder people resist it.

There are other reasons, too, for choosing therapy. In the next chapter, we shall look briefly at those and then set the scene for our practice of self-therapy.

4

Discord: Why you might turn to a therapist

I spoke earlier of feeling the need for *"... expert help: someone to talk to, someone to assist us in navigating our way through stormy waters."* But it is not only stormy waters than can be problematical. Sometimes, the waters are too calm. Feeling becalmed — the sensation of being stuck, of not moving when we think we should be, of boredom, ennui and 'going nowhere' — is also a good reason for seeking help.

Before I became a psychologist — and ultimately a psychotherapist in private practice — I was trained as a social worker. Those first four years of my training were all about helping people solve problems. And because, like hospitals, the funding for the agencies that I worked for was based on 'throughput,' the model I was required to work from was: client has a problem →client seeks help →client receives help →problem solved →client discharged.

Sometimes, that was the way it worked, but not always. This model worked just fine for practical problems like finding accommodation, sorting out household finances, arranging home help and so on. But not all problems were practical ones. Often, when clients came to me for help and we talked about their lives and the issues they were facing, it would turn out that these were mostly *inner* issues — like grief, depression, boredom, yearning, dissatisfaction etc., rather than outer ones. Gradually, as we talked, as we looked at things like people's early experiences, the childhood survival strategies they had developed that may or may not be working well in adulthood, the transitions they might be going through...and so on, we would find ourselves switching models. We would move, imperceptibly, from problem-solving mode into *growth* mode. However, personal and spiritual growth have no end-point. There never comes a time when we can say "There we are, I have now finished growing" because the only time we could truthfully utter those words is immediately *after* our last breath.

Since the growth model did not fit the agencies' guidelines for discharging clients, I often got critical comments from my colleagues. One of the cardinal sins, for a social worker, is having clients become dependent on you. But although many of my clients did depend for a while on my presence in their lives, through working with me they gradually internalized the methods we were using until the time came when they no longer needed to book appointments. Their 'inner therapist' had replaced me, the outer one. They had mastered self-therapy.

A few people, although they will quite readily consult a doctor, a dentist, a lawyer, an acupuncturist etc., seem to think seeking help for psychological/emotional issues is somehow shameful, probably because of the stigma attached to mental illness in our culture. I think this is why so many life coaches have appeared in our midst in recent years. Whereas the word 'therapy' suggests illness or dysfunction, we associate coaches and personal trainers with health and fitness.

Life coaches differentiate themselves from counselors and psychotherapists by saying that counseling and psychotherapy traditionally deal with healing the past and solving problems whereas life coaching focuses on the future and on formulating and attaining goals. For someone wrestling with severe psychological/emotional problems such as clinical depression or someone in danger of harming others or themselves, the choice is clear. Life coaches are not trained to deal with such things. But many people whose real need is for growth-oriented therapy end up seeing traditional counselors and therapists who are working from the same 'hospital' model as those agencies I worked for many years ago, rather than a growth model, especially if a diagnosis of psychopathology is needed before the government or insurance company will agree to foot the bill.

At the same time, any model that focuses only on the your future and your goals without taking a good look at how and why your unconscious mind might be sabotaging those goals, is working with only half the tools in the toolbox. What would be the most useful all round would be a highly trained psychotherapist with not only a growth-oriented approach but also a holistic, transpersonal one. By which I mean a therapist who looks at the *really* big picture: your body, your mind, your thoughts, ideas, goals, emotions and feelings and your soul; you as part of a family, a community, a culture; your spirituality, beliefs, and life lessons and how you relate to the rest of life on the planet.

There are such people around but they are thin on the ground. However, my hope in writing this book is that it will enable you to provide for yourself everything that such a person could give you—and all for the price on the cover!

A note of warning

As I said just now, there are some situations in which outside help is definitely called for. Specifically:

- If you have ever been diagnosed with a mental illness such as schizophrenia or any type of psychosis or personality disorder
- If you are—or have recently been—seriously contemplating suicide
- If you are currently using—or are likely to be using—illegal drugs or abusing legal ones

If you are—or have recently been—harming yourself physically.

I certainly hope you will seek outside help if you feel you really need it. Seeking help with emotional issues is no different from seeing a doctor about physical ones or calling a plumber to fix a leak. As a therapist myself, I have received valuable help from other therapists at certain times in my life and would never discourage anyone from doing so.

If you do decide you need to involve someone else, the choice of who to talk to will be limited to who is available. Remember, though, that anyone who has an established personal relationship with you such as a friend, relative or partner will not be able to remain totally objective and emotionally detached from whatever you want to discuss with them, even if they are professionally trained.

Remember, too, that psychiatrists, whose training is mainly in psychopathology, usually know far more about prescribing drugs than about any other kind of therapy. However, drugs have their uses and in some situations psychiatric treatment can be life-saving.

There are various specializations you might take into account also. For example, hypnotherapists are particularly good at helping people overcome phobias and addictions, such as smoking, as they can speak directly to your unconscious. Cranio-sacral therapists and EFT practitioners work well with anxiety issues. And since most practitioners who work in the various types of complementary medicine — Ayurveda, acupuncture, chiropractic, herbalism, homeopathy, naturopathy etc.—see the body and mind as an integrated whole, any one of those will almost certainly have something to offer. I have tried most of them at some time in my life and all were beneficial. The more different lenses through which we can see ourselves, the better our overall understanding and self-awareness become.

This book is designed both as a stand-alone guide to self-therapy and as an adjunct to any other kind of therapy in which you are—or might become—involved. Much of the content is derived from the 'homework' I used to suggest to my clients when I was a practicing psychotherapist.

From reading through—and hopefully pondering on—this first section, you have assembled the material a therapist would need in getting to know who you are and how you tick. So let's get down to business.

PART II

THE ART AND SKILL OF

SELF-THERAPY

5

Setting the Scene

Whenever you go to meet a therapist you enter a special kind of space. This space has both an outer attribute and an inner attribute. Its outer attribute is that it is usually a private, self-enclosed physical space — an office with comfortable chairs, a consulting room — in which you and the therapist can work together for a certain period of time in total privacy.

Its inner attribute is similar. But instead of being defined by walls, closed doors and silent telephones, this inner space is made safe by the conscious intent of the therapist. It is as though she or he is able to spin a cocoon of warmth, safety and confidentiality around you so that you feel able to relax and go inwards. In a sense, you can become a child again for a while, unconcerned with the affairs of the outside world, safe in the knowledge that an adult is caring for you.

If the cocoon is strong enough, it alone can make you safe, even in the absence of physical walls. (I have sat with a client on a park bench and created a cocoon around us.) So doing self-therapy does not require building an extension on to your house. And since you are your only client you don't have to make appointments or to work in fifty-minute hours. You can do it anywhere, any time and in sessions of any length. The only requirement is that you do it deliberately, consciously and with full attention and that you create the sort of inner safe space that makes it possible and easy.

My own venue of choice for self-therapy sessions is actually the great outdoors. Luckily I live in the country and can walk for hours without meeting a soul, or stop to hold hands with a fern, ask questions of a tree, talk to a bird or sit on a log for a while if I feel like it. But I have also developed the ability to talk to myself very quietly and without moving my lips so that if necessary I can do some self-therapy exercises while walking around the city or even on a train without attracting anyone's attention.

First task: Enlist your two primary helpers

Self-therapy is a team effort. There are three main roles and you have to play all three of them. So your first task is to get to know your two primary team mates. These are the Observing Self (shortened to OS from now on) and the Virtual Therapist (VT). Think of yourself as the team leader, whose task it is to co-ordinate the work, schedule the sessions and put the results into practice. Like a research scientist, you are discovering new information, interviewing experts, designing experiments and using the results wisely, in this case to heal wounds, to evolve spiritually and to improve the quality of your life.

The Observing Self

This is a key part of self-therapy. Having an OS means developing a certain kind of specialized attention. Remember, the task of the OS is merely to observe and record without judging or interfering. It operates exactly like CCTV, giving you real-time feedback about what is going on within and around you and recording it in case you need to refer to it later.

To develop the OS, the most important thing you have to do is pay attention and watch. It is as though you set aside a tiny bit of yourself whose sole job it is to watch everything that happens, while the rest of you gets on and lives life. Watch what arises in your thoughts, feelings and emotions, moment by moment. Listen to what you say (face to face or on the phone) or write (including email and texts) to others and how you feel as you say or write it. See what effect it has on the other and how you feel about the other's reaction.

Notice when you are reacting (out of your feelings, emotions, opinions etc.), rather than thoughtfully *responding*.

Notice when you are making inward judgments on a person, a statement, a situation.

Just observe. Remember, the Observing Self is merely that—an impartial observer. What you do with those observations is a separate thing, just as the CCTV camera is separate from the person who scans the screen.

Watch how feelings can arise from thoughts and vice versa. Notice where your mind usually goes when it leaves the present moment—which most people's minds tend to do, over and over again throughout the day.

Here is a practice exercise

Pick a time when you can sit quietly for ten minutes, undisturbed.

Get into a comfortable position and relax.

Close your eyes and let your thoughts drift wherever they want to go.

Switch your full attention to the process and start to observe and record everything that happens within and around you.

Now, as each thought, idea, feeling or whatever arises in your mind, give it a one-word label and say the word aloud. It may sound something like this:

"Silly...itching...memory...shopping...telephone...impatience...pain...bird...memory...tune...thirsty...siren...memory...leg...breathing..." and so on.

Notice how you switch between awareness of your body, awareness of your surroundings and awareness of your inner process. Notice how images call up other images and memories lead you away from the 'now.' Notice how unfinished tasks nudge you, how painful memories attempt to swamp you or happy ones tempt you away on nostalgic mental journeys. Notice your tendency to re-hash the past and to rehearse the future instead of remaining in the here-and-now. Notice whether you are thinking in words or in pictures or a mixture of both.

Above all, notice whether you are making judgments about all of this or merely observing it. If you find yourself judging, quickly label it 'judgment' and move on.

Before you bring this practice session to an end, say thank-you to yourself for taking time out for self-therapy. It is important to express your gratitude because every bit of self-therapy you do is a gift to yourself. And, since the better you understand and accept yourself the easier it becomes to understand and accept other people, what you are doing now is a gift to them also, albeit in a round-about sort of way.

Later, try the same exercise in other settings, such as walking along the street, sitting in a parked car or on a bus or train with people around you.

The Virtual Therapist

Creating the VT is easier than you think. This is how you do it:

Imagine the absolutely perfect listener—someone who will listen fully, intently and compassionately to everything and anything you say to him or her, without criticism, judgment or blame and will respond with unconditional love, respect and kindness. It is just like when you were a child and invented imaginary friends. Those friends felt real to you. Your VT will soon feel very real as well. The way to bring your VT to life is to start acting the role of that wonderful listener and to do it as authentically as you possibly can. Begin by feeling yourself into the therapist role. You, as the therapist, have a responsibility to care for your client, just as you would care for a child or a puppy. Imagine yourself standing outside yourself, feeling protective and loving. Remember *never* to be critical when in the role of the therapist. Always be kind. Always have total compassion for your 'client.' Once you have felt yourself into the role of the VT, you can try asking your client a few simple, gentle questions in order to elicit what it is that needs working on first. It is like when you walk into your doctor's surgery and the doctor looks up and (hopefully) smiles and says "What brings you here today?"

Your answers to your VT may possibly be based on something your OS has noticed. Or they may arise directly, from things that have been niggling you lately, things that have been on some mental gotta-sort-that-out list. Once you select a topic, the dialogue between you and your VT can begin.

From now on, in these sessions, you will be working as though you are two people. It may take you a while to get the hang of that. However, most of us, especially as children, have had experience in playing roles and some of us even got to play multiple roles, so think back to school plays, Christmas pageants or whatever and revive your innate skills at role-playing and shape-shifting. It may help, at first, to move your position as you switch from one role to the other (we shall be doing something similar in later chapters as we explore ways of resolving issues with third parties and bringing to life our inner 'cast of thousands,' so playing several roles in one play is a key technique in self-therapy).

All your virtual therapist will ever do is listen, ask kind but probing questions, encourage you to go deeper, occasionally sum up for you, keep you on track with the topic and reassure you that the process you are engaging in is not only *not* crazy but actually saner than sane.

Here are some of the useful phrases your therapist might use:

"What is bothering you most about your life at the moment?"
"Can you explain more to me about that?"
"What are you feeling right now?"
"Can you tell me more about this feeling?" "Whereabouts in your body do you feel this most intensely?" "Pretend you are only seven years old. If you were just to blurt out what you really, truly feel/think/want right now, what would you say?" "Does this remind you of anything? When have you felt like this before?" "Is there a familiar pattern happening here?" "What does your inner child have to say about this?" "Can you tell me your ideas about what might need to change and how we might set about changing it?"

NB: The question after this last one should always be: "Before we talk more about how you might make that change, please also tell me about the part of you that doesn't want to make that change." If changing was straightforward, you would have done it already so you can make a bet that there is a part of you resisting that change. Getting in touch with that part is a key technique in therapy because once you do, the two parts can dialogue and (hopefully) come to some agreement. We shall return to this in Chapter 8.

As you answer the questions, you will most likely find that you and your VT have slightly different voices. Over time, these may differentiate even more. In any case, when you have this kind of dialogue, take the process slowly and thoughtfully and remain fully attentive.

An important question about sabotage

As I mentioned before, we all have resistance to therapy, even self-therapy. When we start discovering some Shadow stuff that embarrasses us, it is easier to stop going to sessions and dismiss the therapy as ineffective (or in this case, decide this book is not worth the money) than it is to hang in there. So whenever you start a new piece of inner work, have your VT ask "How might you sabotage this?"

Once you have established the VT as an entity you can consult him/her whenever there is anything about yourself or your life that you need help in exploring.

Teamwork

You, your OS and your VT are going to be working as a team of three, all of whom will always be present. Your role, like that of the security guard who keeps an eye on the CCTV, is to notice when something is happening that might need some action taken. This may or may not need the assistance of your VT, but the VT needs to remain on standby, ready to be called on whenever help is needed. You and/or the VT will both be able to call in other helpers from time to time. One such helper is the Nurturing Parent (NP)

Role of the Nurturing Parent

There are times when the NP alone can achieve miracles. The example that always comes to mind is what happened with Ralph.

Ralph re-parents himself

Ralph was a big, burly fireman who prided himself on his toughness. Abandoned as a toddler, his childhood survival strategy had been to close in on himself emotionally and 'tough it out' as a loner.

This strategy got him through childhood but by the time

he came to see me, at the age of 34, it was causing problems. After three years of trying to find a way inside Ralph's shell and achieve some real intimacy, his girlfriend had finally left him and her leaving, triggering as it did his deeply buried feelings of abandonment, had plunged him into a deep depression.

On Ralph's third visit to my office, as he sat slumped disconsolately in the chair, I picked up the thick sweater that he had been wearing when he came in, folded it and placed it in his arms. I asked him to close his eyes, hold the sweater to his chest and imagine it was a baby boy whose mother had abandoned him on the doorstep of an orphanage. He did as I asked and there was silence for a while. Then suddenly, clutching the sweater tightly against him, Ralph cried out "Oh you poor little bastard!" and tears began to stream down his face for the first time in two decades.

From that point on, Ralph realized that he could use his Nurturing Parent self to take care of the abandoned child that still lived within him. He told me, some weeks later, "Now, whenever I feel lost and lonely, I just give myself a little secret pat on my chest, like this" and with his right hand he gently patted a spot just over his heart. It was his private message from himself to himself that said "It's OK. I love you. You are not alone." Not only that, but learning through therapy to understand his feelings and express them stood him in good stead when it came to another relationship. The last time I heard from Ralph was when he wrote to tell me he was getting married.

We can all benefit from self-parenting. So let your NP talk to your Child. Praise him or her for the adaptive strategies s/he created and promise that if any of those strategies have become a problem in adulthood they can safely be let go of now. Promise that you will always be there, caring, comforting, listening and supporting.

6

Problem-solving

What brings most people to therapy in the first place is usually some sort of problem, and the same often applies with self-therapy.

Problems in an office, laboratory or workshop can frequently be solved by pure, logical reasoning, and sometimes personal problems can be solved that way too so that is where the following, highly effective problem-solving formula begins. For this first step, switch on your Adult ego state and grab a pencil and paper.

Step 1

Brainstorm. This means write down every possible solution you can possibly think of, including the crazy, way-out and illegal ones (especially the crazy, way-out and illegal ones because just listing them helps to switch on your creativity, believe it or not.) *Don't evaluate any solutions at this stage.* Not even a little bit. Just list everything you can think of. When you are totally done, proceed to Step 2.

Step 2

Go through the longlist, evaluating it as you go and crossing things off till you end up with a workable shortlist. Repeat this process several times if necessary, looking at all the pros and cons, rating them and comparing scores if you need to, until your solution becomes really clear or there is a tie between two options.

Step 3

Now it is time to take intuition, gut feelings and the other two ego states into account. Some solutions *feel* more right than others, even if the numbers don't stack up quite as well. This is where you might need to move on to some of the other tools in your self-therapy toolkit and we shall be looking at those next. Your Adult may have been able to solve the problem by the pencil and paper method but you also need to consult your inner Child and your inner Parent, so that your Adult can factor these in. This is because:

—whatever solution you come up with has to have Parental approval. In other words, it has to fit with your personal value system, your morals and the standards you have set for yourself
—your Inner Child has to feel happy about it otherwise it won't work.

Sometimes, with a bit more work by the Adult, and taking into account the opinions of the Parent and the Child, you might come up with some sort of composite solution that everyone is happy with.

Ideally, let some time elapse before a final decision is made so that you can sleep on it, notice what comes up in your dreams and daydreams, examine any further doubts or ideas that pop up. Consensus tends usually to be a slow and laborious process, and an inner consensus between the various aspects of your psyche is no exception. But decisions reached by consensus are usually easier to stick to and everyone's commitment to them is usually high.

Step 4

Once a decision has been reached, make sure that you (a)

are totally clear on how the solution is going to be implemented and (b) have worked out how the results are going to be evaluated and when. Remember that your Parent and Child selves need to play a part in the evaluation process also.

Conflict resolution

Office mates find a solution

Neville, June and Sandra, who all shared an office, were conflicted about the window. Neville, who usually arrived first each morning, used to open the window wide to get rid of the stale air and smell. Sandra, whose desk was near the window, always shut the window angrily when she found it open, glaring at Neville and muttering about the cold and the draught. June, who suffered from asthma, complained that the opening and shutting of the window and the consequent changes in temperature made her wheezy and also said the bickering upset her.

Their problem-solving had stalled because they were all so fixated on what they didn't want. But if someone had taken the process up a notch and asked them what they *did* want, it would have turned out that they wanted the same thing — a peaceful, pleasant working environment with good-quality air. Comparing positive needs instead of negative ones can often yield a creative solution. In this case, it happened by accident.

June, leafing through a product catalogue for allergy sufferers one day, discovered a gadget you could plug in which would cleanse the air of particulates, odors and almost all airborne pollutants. This, she realized, would suit everyone's needs. Sandra wouldn't have to sit in a draught, Neville wouldn't have to endure smelly stale air and for her it would certainly help her breathing. They put in a request to the boss and got one. So the problem that had appeared insoluble actually wasn't.

Reframing a problem in terms of positive needs instead of negative grumbles doesn't always yield a happy solution but it is always worth trying.

If problem-solving doesn't work...

When you think about all the complexities of a human being—conscious/unconscious, inner cast of characters, left and right cerebral hemispheres, body, mind and spirit—it is hardly surprising that there are times when this rational, logical problem-solving approach alone simply does not do the trick and you need to move on to the more advanced self-therapy techniques we shall be covering next.

7

Personal Growth

Although it is often a problem of some sort that can bring you into therapy, it soon becomes clear that many of the techniques you discover in the therapy room can be used for the rest of your life as tools for your personal growth as an evolving human being. This is even more true of self-therapy. Once you have acquired these tools and begun to use them, you will find yourself turning to them automatically in all sorts of situations.

Coded messages from your unconscious mind can turn up at any moment, for example in dreams, and you will find yourself eager to decode them (see Chapter 9).

There are various other ways that messages may come and you will soon find yourself looking out for them. Here are four to watch for.

Notice OTT reactions
Do you ever find yourself suddenly reacting much more strongly and emotionally than the situation seems to warrant? Over-the-top emotional reactions are a sure sign that a deep nerve in you has been touched. Watch for these OTT reactions in your everyday life, and if one happens, take the next available opportunity to discuss it with your VT. Trace it back to its true origins (often in childhood).

Notice substitutions
Many of us habitually plaster over unbearable feelings with slightly more bearable ones. If we grew up in a family where anger was unacceptable, for example, whenever we feel anger we might speedily replace it with sadness or

depression so as to hide it from ourselves. Some people paste laughter on top of the urge to weep. Teasing is frequently a cover for hostility.

It is easier to spot substitutions in other people than in ourselves, but if you are observant, you might catch a tiny glimpse of an original feeling, just before it gets covered over. Then with your VT's help you can explore what is going on.

Notice what your body is saying

The body speaks its mind

Roger sits with his legs crossed and appears quite calm except that I notice his right foot is swinging. I address his foot directly. I ask the foot what it is saying and the foot (through Roger) replies that it would really like to kick somebody. Only then does Roger start to get in touch with some anger he has been trying to suppress.

Claire is absent-mindedly playing with her wedding ring, sliding it on and off her finger. When I encourage her hands to speak, they start voicing Claire's doubts about her marriage—doubts she had been trying not to admit into consciousness.

Our bodies often express what is still hidden in our unconscious minds, so pay attention to anything yours might be trying to tell you about what is really going on.[5]

Owning your projections

An important concept in therapy is what Jung called the Shadow. We all have one of these. It is the disowned, 'unlived' part of ourselves. In the Shadow is our potential for doing, saying and feeling things which we cannot allow ourselves consciously to do or feel or say. The Shadow versions of ourselves are often selves we would dislike and be ashamed of and/or embarrassed by if we knew they actually existed. Or they are aspects of ourselves that were dangerous to exhibit in childhood because they would have been frowned on, even though another family might have seen them as positive. For instance I once had a client who was ashamed of her preoccupation with cleanliness and tidiness because as a little girl growing up in a messy household she had been cruelly teased about it. All the things in our Shadow are things we want to hide, so we deny the possibility of their existence altogether, even to ourselves. When we were constructing an identity for ourselves, the public face we want the world to see, which Jung called the Persona (originally a word that meant 'mask') these were the elements we left out.

However, when we spot these things in other people, we get very judgmental about them. "How could he do such a thing?" we exclaim, with huge indignation. "He just walked off and left the project in the middle and left everyone else to finish it. How selfish. How thoughtless…" Or "Look at her, showing off, up there making a spectacle of herself…how disgraceful." Our own unconscious minds are fully screening from view our own potential for selfishness and thoughtlessness, our own occasional longing to quit something and walk away, our own yearning to perform and be seen etc. and projecting it safely on to someone else. When we do that, what we are actually projecting is our own inner Shadow. Whenever you notice yourself having an unusually strong reaction to someone else's behavior — either positive or negative but more often the latter — there is a good chance that some kind of projection is happening.

So part of getting to know yourself better is getting to know your Shadow self. Noticing your projections is one way to do that. Look for those times when you find yourself becoming unusually irritated by someone else's behavior and ask yourself if it is possible that a projection is involved. Is there a Shadow part of you that would display that same behavior if it dared? Another way to discover the Shadow is to look for it in your dreams. The Shadow will often be represented by a dark figure or someone you can't quite see.

Once you spot a projection, the next step is to own it. Say to yourself "Yes, there is actually a part of me which is like that." And that is perfectly OK.

There actually is no behavior that is totally inappropriate under any circumstances. I am no murderer but if my child was being strangled and the only way to save her life was to plunge a carving knife into the strangler's back, I would do it without hesitation. Like tools in a toolshed, some behaviors are in daily use while others rarely or never get taken off their hooks. But they are there. Re-owning your own projections is quite safe because what is important is not *owning* the tools in your shed; it is whether and when and how you *use* them that matters.

Accepting the Shadow as part of who we are is an important step in the individuation process—the process of becoming more fully ourselves.

8

The Magic of Chairs

(Note: if you have physical difficulties with moving around, please read this chapter anyway; the note at the end will explain how to do the same exercises without chairs.)

Of all the tools one might use in self-therapy, and by far the most useful, is the chair. Not a special kind of chair, just a chair. Any chair will do, and you need more than one. A chair is like a blank page: you can fill it with anything. When my children were little, we had something called the 'boredom chair.' If ever one of them announced that she was bored (no doubt hoping for a pick-up game of 'Why Don't You? Yes but…') I simply directed her to the boredom chair and suggested that she sit on it and do nothing until the boredom disappeared — which it invariably did, usually within a few seconds.

In self-therapy, we use chairs for monologues, for dialogues or for discussion groups.

Monologues

These are the therapy of choice whenever you have a problem with ambivalence. Part of you is feeling one way about the issue and another part is feeling another way and there is a tussle going on inside. It is hard to make a decision. There are pros and cons and you could argue it either way, so which outcome do you *really* want? OK, here is how you proceed.

Set out two chairs, either back to back or facing in fairly different directions but not facing each other. Now sit in

Chair 1 and speak, as fully and eloquently as you can, in favor of *just one* of the arguments. Really make a case for Option 1, as though you are trying to convince someone else that this is the right way to go. When you have finished speaking, spend a few moments being really super-aware of how you are feeling, especially in your body.

Now get up and switch to Chair 2. Completely ignoring everything the first 'speaker' said, launch into a full and eloquent exposition of the *other* argument. Make a really good case for Option 2. Once again, spend some time checking out how you feel.

Switch back to the first chair. Once again, speak fully in favor of Option 1. This time try to be aware of your feelings even while you are still speaking. Then go to Chair 2 and do the same thing for Option 2.

You may need to switch back and forth a number of times until you have fine-tuned your awareness enough to pick up subtle differences in the feeling tone between the two chairs. But after a while, one of three things will happen:

—the exercise will have revealed to you that you are not really as ambivalent as you thought you were and that one of these two options feels better than the other and is actually the one you deep-down favor

—you will have had a brainwave about how the best of each might be combined into a third option that you like even better than either of them

—despite moving between the chairs a number of times, the scales remain totally evenly balanced.

If the latter is the case, then answer this question: is there a deadline for this decision?

If the answer is no, then the right decision is almost certainly to leave things as they are for now and stay with the ambivalence. Ambivalence almost always resolves over time, and you need to give it whatever time it needs.

If the answer is yes, there is a deadline and you *have* to decide right now but the scales appear to remain at 50%/50%, then find a coin, decide which side represents which option and tell yourself you will act according to the result of the coin toss. This alone will be enough to flush out any lurking feelings that didn't reveal themselves during the two-chair exercise. (There is nothing like having a gun at your head to make you realize what really matters to you and what doesn't!)

You can of course use this exercise for more options than just two. You just need more chairs and more time. And in the unlikely event that you end up evenly balanced between multiple options, instead of a coin toss you will need to mark some pieces of paper with the options, shuffle them, place them upside down and then choose one without looking.

Some people, when they are facing difficult decisions, turn to various divination methods. They may, for example throw coins and consult the I Ching. They may do a Tarot spread or read tea leaves (a method you hear little about in this age of teabags) or a swing a pendulum over those pieces of paper I just mentioned. They also look for what appear to be significant 'signs' in the world around them. If you are not familiar with any of these methods you might suppose they are ways of getting answers from some mysterious outside source. In fact they are not. Since you would be using your own mind to interpret whatever you learn from these sources, they are merely mirrors that reflect, in very subtle ways, what your unconscious mind is trying to say on the matter. By enabling you to read coded messages from you to yourself, the solo use of any of these methods can be seen as a useful extension of your self-therapy toolkit. (Note that I said 'solo use.' The above comments don't apply if a third party is doing the interpreting.)

When difficult decisions have to be made, let's also remember which of our inner cast of characters needs to be consulted. As mentioned earlier, Adult, Parent and Child all have to sign off on important decisions or problems will arise later.

Dialogues

The wonderful thing about self-therapy is that as well as having discussions between various parts of yourself you can also invite anyone you choose to join in, regardless of where in the world they live or whether they are alive or dead.

(If the idea of chatting to dead people seems a little odd to you, remember that it is considered perfectly normal behavior by all those millions of folks who regularly chat to Allah, Jesus, Mary, Mohammed, Buddha or any one of a vast number of saints and bodhisattvas no longer incarnate.)

Two-chair dialogue with another (virtual) person

This can be used for any situation in which there are things you need to say to another person but for one reason or another have not been able to say to them directly. This could be, for example, one of your parents, your boss, a sibling, a friend or acquaintance. It could be somebody from your past or somebody you are currently in some kind of relationship with. It works especially well when you are feeling emotionally blocked by unfinished business with a person who is no longer around—or someone who is alive and well but who you are not able or willing to face directly with your feelings, such as a boss who has the power to fire you.

People often use it for saying goodbye to someone who has died, particularly if the death was sudden and there was no opportunity to say it at the time. If there is someone no longer in your life to whom you are still emotionally clinging, it can be a powerful way of letting go of them and wishing them well. I have also seen many people use the two-chair method to express a long-held rage against an oppressive figure from their childhood, though in some cases their inner Child still had so much fear that it took weeks to muster enough courage to do the exercise.

Place two chairs more or less facing each other. Sit in one of the chairs. Close your eyes for a few moments. Relax and breathe slowly until you feel really comfortable.

Now open your eyes, look across at the other chair and visualize, in that chair, whoever it is that you want to talk to. Try to see them as clearly as you can. Notice what they are wearing, how their hair is arranged, where their hands are, what shoes they have on…and so on. Keep visualizing until you have a very clear vision of that person sitting there waiting for you to speak.

Once it feels as though the person is really there, start talking to them. Tell them how you feel. Tell them whatever is in your heart or on your mind that needs to be said. Notice how you feel. If there are any emotions attached to your words, let them come freely through. Go on talking until you feel as though you have fully expressed whatever it was you wanted to say.

Often, just being able to express the feelings out loud is enough to make this a satisfying exercise and nothing more is needed. Sometimes, however, it develops into a dialogue. In which case:

Listen for the reply from the Other.

Let the Other know what feelings their reply has brought up in you.

Listen again for their reply.

...and so on.

Such a dialogue may be useful, as it may give you a better understanding of the Other's point of view. There is of course a danger that it may turn into ineffectual bickering. If this happens, a therapist skilled in chairwork would usually intervene at that point and may 'interview' the Other as to his or her feelings and motivations. You would be asked to take the role of the Other and speak out of *their* life experience. It is amazing how much we unconsciously know about why others speak and act the way they do.

Terry and Carl

Terry's childhood was made continually miserable by a psychologically abusive stepfather called Carl who bullied him constantly. When, at the age of 42, he put Carl in the chair and yelled at him, letting go into all the impotent rage he had held back for so many years, all he could hear was Carl yelling right back, still abusing him and putting him down the way he always had. But when I had Terry sit in Carl's chair and interviewed him as 'Carl' it was revealed that Carl himself was actually a man with very low self-esteem who himself had been bullied by his own father and two aggressive older brothers. When the session was over, although Terry still disliked his stepfather, his dislike was now tinged with a modicum of compassion and his rage had considerably abated. (Interestingly, while Terry was 'being' Carl, his expression and body language changed. I noticed him alternately clenching and stretching his right hand—a mannerism I had never noticed before. Later, when I mentioned this to Terry he was quite surprised. "Dad used to do that all the time," he said. "I'd completely forgotten that till now.")

It is perfectly possible to have one's own VT do just what I did with 'Carl' and do a two-chair dialogue between the VT and the Other. Deliberately putting oneself in the role of the Other and 'walking a mile in their moccasins' is always helpful in any situation where there is conflict.

The three-letter exercise

Instead of — or as well as — using chairs to resolve unfinished business with an Other, another very effective technique is to write three letters. Write them all out, fully, either in longhand or printed out from your computer.

The first letter is from you to the Other, explaining what the unresolved problem is.

The second letter is from the Other to you. It is the letter you think you would be likely to receive from that person in response.

The third is also from the Other but it is the one you long to receive. The loving, healing one that makes you weep for joy.

Read all the letters through again slowly, in the same order you wrote them.

Now fold them carefully together, in two, then four...

...and then ritually burn them and go wash your hands.

This exercise works at a deep, unconscious level and even if you don't feel the effects right away, they will still be happening.

Two-chair dialogue between aspects of yourself

The figure in the opposite chair can just as easily be a part of yourself—your inner Child, for example, your inner Parent or your inner Critic or Saboteur. This time, however, since both are equally part of you, you are going to move back and forth between the chairs, speaking for each part in turn.

It is vitally important to keep the chairs separate. If you are speaking from your Child, make sure you are sitting in the Child chair. As soon as you start hearing the voice of the Parent, jump up and sit in the Parent chair and speak from there.

Or even more chairs...

When the Adult (A) you decides to do chairwork, since the Nurturing Parent (NP) and the Critical Parent (CP) have different voices and both may want to say their piece—and even the Natural Child (NC) and Adapted Child (AC) parts of you might have different sorts of input—you might find yourself needing more chairs. (Or if some speakers choose to stand, perch on a desk or sit on the floor, that is fine, but keep track of them and, once again, remember to sit, stand or perch in the right place for whichever 'self' is speaking.)

A "Let's all get together and discuss the problem." (Switch chairs)
NC "I need a vacation." (Switch chairs)
NP "Of course you do, darling." (Switch chairs)
CP "But you haven't worked hard enough." (Switch chairs)
AC "No, I don't deserve a vacation yet." (Switch chairs)
A "AC, why do you think NC doesn't deserve a vacation?" (Switch chairs)
AC "Because..." and so on.

(As you can see, chairwork has the side benefit of getting you plenty of exercise!)

Your cast of thousands

In Chapter 1 we looked at the so-called 'ego states' – your two kinds of Inner Parent, two kinds of Inner Child and the rational Adult who is the one you are most likely to identify as the Real You. We have also mentioned the Inner Critic that resides within most of us. This part of us is often closely allied with (or even identical with) the Critical Parent, but since it may originally have been based not on an actual parent but on someone else, for example a sibling or an authority figure such as a teacher, we shall treat it here as a distinctly separate part of your psyche.

You have almost certainly met—or at least heard—this Inner Critic from time to time. And even if you have not met your Inner Saboteur you have probably witnessed the results of his or her determination to mess something up for you.

The key to working successfully with all these inner parts, which are often referred to as 'sub-personalities' is to understand their big secret and in a minute I shall tell you what their secret is. (I know what it is because all sub-personalities guard the very same secret.) First, though, let's create a setting in which they can all make themselves known to you.

An American psychotherapist called Virginia Satir, who died in 1988, used to invite her clients to hold what she called a 'parts party.' This is where you invite all these different part of yourself to come together in the same place and discuss their roles.

Here again, we can make use of chairs. However, if there are not enough chairs, don't worry. You could just as easily have a hippie sort of party where everybody sits around on the floor.

Jenny's Conference

Jenny decided that something really had to change. Her study was full of papers that needed filing, the garden badly needed weeding, the dog was overdue for his shots, her email in-box was full and she hadn't phoned her mother in two weeks. The publisher she worked for had just sent two more manuscripts for proof-reading and she still hadn't finished the last one. After she had seen the children off on the school bus she made a cup of tea and picked up the novel she was reading and the next thing she knew it was nearly noon. She was very angry with herself. "There I go again. Wasting time when I have so much to do." This sort of thing was happening more and more. It was as though the various parts of Jenny were at war with each other. So Jenny decided to hold a peace conference.

Her first step was to isolate each of her warring parts and give it a name and some characteristics.

The Office Manager, who wore sensible shoes and spectacles, had a very critical manner and reveled in orderliness and routines, came in accusing Jenny of being a lazy slob.

The Gardener. who wore old clothes and had mud under her fingernails, loved animals and disliked being cooped up indoors, was cross about having to attend the conference so stared out of the window and ignored everyone in the room.

The Natural Child, a dreamer who loved to curl up on the couch with a book, had a paperback with her and was surreptitiously reading it.

The Worker, who did the proof-reading and dealt with the deadlines, was grumbling about having to leave the computer and was glaring at the Natural Child.

The Playmate, who enjoyed chatting with friends on

Facebook, was a bit defensive.

The Adapted Child, whose mother had always been prone to depressive episodes, looked worried and anxious.

Jenny's VT welcomed everyone and asked them each to speak about who they were, what bothered them and what they wanted Jenny to do about it. Once they had all done that, it was time to uncover their big secret, which was that *they were all, without exception, doing what they did out of love.* So she asked them each in turn to explain to Jenny the ways in which they each showed their love and concern for her. They thought awhile and then answered.

The Office Manager said, "I care for you by reminding you how you should behave (just like your Dad used to) and by keeping everything neat so you'll know where it is and not panic."

The Gardener said, "I take care of you by helping you use your creativity, bringing you joy and keeping you in touch with the rest of Nature."

The Natural Child said, "My job is to make sure you relax and enjoy life."

The Worker said, "Without me, you would go broke."

The Playmate said, "Without me, you'd be lonely and friendless like you were when you first started high school."

The Adapted Child said, "If she (meaning Jenny's mother) gets depressed, we'll all suffer so I protect you by reminding you to be a good girl and keep her happy." (The VT stepped in at this point to do a reality check and it turned out that Jenny's mother used to suffer depressive episodes every month but hadn't had one since she got through menopause twenty years ago.)

Once she had heard all this and realized what their underlying intentions were, Jenny expressed her gratitude to them all and asked each of them how they would like her to honor these intentions. She asked them all to help her make changes in a way that would create more harmony between everyone in the room. By the end of the session they were all chatting and being friendly and co-operative and Jenny had worked out a schedule for herself which ensured that all her inner selves would get their needs met in the fairest way possible. Now, any time Jenny finds herself starting into negative self-talk she recalls that conference and it helps her to stop.

Journaling and other chairless techniques

All the techniques using chairs can also be accomplished in other ways. If you are in a wheelchair, simply move your chair to different positions. Or set up a tabletop scene using suitable small objects such as little toys, model figures, different-shaped pebbles and so on to represent the different speakers.

You can also explore issues in a similar way using pen and paper instead, as though you were writing a play. It is slower that way, but works equally well. For dialogues, use different pens to represent the different speakers if you are writing longhand or different fonts/colors if you are typing.

Using a written journal for self-therapy is a tried and trusted technique and there are many books written about it. It is particularly useful for recording and working with dreams, which we are going to look at in the next chapter

So you see, any of the techniques in this book can be creatively adapted in ways that make them suitable for anyone, regardless of any physical limitations.

9

Working with Dreams

In this chapter, we shall be learning about dreams by using the example of an actual dream and what it helped the dreamer to discover.

Ann's Dream—August 12—Moon waxing.

"This dream," says Ann, "struck me with such force that I wrote it down. I've been writing many of my dreams down ever since.

I was inside some sort of walled city in a desert. High walls, sandstone/adobe. It was night-time, but light enough to see clearly and to see the colors as you would in an Henri Rousseau painting of the night.

I was in an alleyway off the main street and there was a kitten / young cat nearby.

Some sort of contretemps was going on. A woman—the leader of a group—dressed like an Arab, complete with turban, swept down the street past me followed by a large group. I don't know if they were guards or just her followers.

Then I was outside the city, in the desert. It was still night time and the colors were beautiful, pale sand and deep blue moonlit sky. I'm looking across at the city. I seem to be moving past it quite fast. But it is camouflaged and I know this. I can see how it looks like a huge hill or mountain rising from the flat desert, with cliffs and gullies etched in the sand and stone that it is covered in to make a disguise.

I am aware of singing. Is it me? Or the stars? Or is it someone singing to me?

Switch to hill-top village, with a man and woman either parting or going down to the desert city. Are they singing to each other?"

A friend asked Ann what part of herself she thought the dream might represent. Ann says:

"I came to the conclusion that the woman was a part of myself which has been unacknowledged for a long time, or rather the lid has been kept on her. It is something to do with power.

"I can't work out the significance of the cat—unless it is a guide.

"I wondered if the hidden city was some sort of symbol for my higher self, with the man and woman being possibly the male and female parts of myself. Perhaps it is part of life's task to integrate these aspects of the self, and maybe the singing represented the harmony which ensues from such an integration. Maybe that's why they were going from the hill village to the hidden city.

"They are just my thoughts on the dream. It was very vivid—my dreams often are—and it is the oddest one I have ever had."

Ann had mentioned to me, earlier, that she had experienced a cancer scare. So I found the following comments of hers highly significant:

"I realized, when I found out I had the 'delinquent cells,' that I've always felt somehow invincible. That I could forge through things somehow, and sort them out. (That woman in the desert!!) I wondered what I had to learn from the experience, and decided that perhaps it was to be vulnerable, and to allow others to help me, albeit whilst still doing my best to help myself. One of the wonderful effects has not been on me, but my husband. He has never been a very demonstrative man, but it was as if he was suddenly allowed to show his feelings— almost as if a dam had burst—very disconcerting at first (I started to think the doctors had told him I was worse than they'd said!) but truly wonderful. What is also wonderful is the fact that the cancer cells had completely disappeared when the histology results came back. The consultant actually phoned me up to tell me and kept wishing me a Happy Christmas."

This is a beautiful dream, and obviously very meaningful. It is what the dream experts call a 'big dream.'

Big dreams

Big dreams are not necessarily epics, or even dramatic. Their bigness lies in the fact that they have a certain quality that almost forces us to remember them, write them down and work with them. (*"This dream struck me with such force that I wrote it down."*)

Carl Jung, in his autobiography, *Memories, Dreams, Reflections*, tells of a childhood dream that was still vivid when he was an old man, and which did not reveal its full meaning to him for many decades. Most of us have had dreams like that. We remember them clearly upon waking, they stay with us a long time and they seem to pulsate with meaning, even though our logical minds often have no clue as to what that meaning might be. Ann's dream was like that. And although she tried to figure it out at the time, and at least one image seemed to have a message for her (the powerful woman in the turban) it was years before the full import of the dream started to come clear.

By creating the image of the high-walled city, Ann's unconscious already knew that her feelings of invincibility were actually a defense against something. And it dropped a sweet little clue about what was being protected inside that defended city. (What better image for vulnerability than a kitten?) Ann did not realize all of that at the time. It was only when the cancer scare happened and she did some deep work around that, that she uncovered her fear of becoming vulnerable—to life, to relationship. It is a fear that most of us share.

Ann's dream signaled to her that she was capable of moving outside of her defended state (going outside the walls into the desert) and quite quickly, too. (Remember how she was *"moving fast"*?) And it was not scary out there either, but quite beautiful. But her conscious mind, at that time, was still 'in the dark' about it. Her defenses were *"camouflaged,"* patterned to look like their surroundings in order *"to make a disguise."* So she is hiding her vulnerability from the world. And her dream is hiding from her. But she is uncovering it (*"it is camouflaged and I know this"*).

The cancer scare came as a surprise, yet inside the city there seems to have been some hint of trouble to come (*"Some sort of contretemps was going on"*) and whatever it was would involve the powerful woman. But the woman had others around her, and Ann said later how supportive other people were when the cancer scare happened.

We might have wondered why the sudden switch of scene to the man and woman on the hill-top, possibly singing to each other in the starlight, had Ann not told us about the sudden switch that took her relationship with her husband to a higher level (the hill-top village?).

Since the dream ends with the man and woman either parting or heading down towards town, it could be that Ann and her husband have now parted from their old ways of relating to each other and after singing together on the hill (delighting in the greater closeness) are now in the process of grounding this new intimacy in new ways of living their daily life together (moving down into the city). However, as Ann so rightly says, the man and woman in the dream may also be the masculine and feminine parts of her, learning to harmonize better. That is one of the wonderful things about dreams: they have onion-like layers, each layer valid in its own right, and all of them saturated with meaning.

Interpreting dreams: a personal code

Ann's friend asked her the essential question that started off her journey of understanding: "What does the woman represent to you?"

Another question might have been "Who does she remind you of?" followed by "What attributes do you tend to associate with that person?" The friend obviously knew that the people and symbols in a dream are unique to the dreamer. Our unconscious minds use our own, personal symbols as their code. If I dream of a snake or a boat or my cousin George, the important thing is not the qualities generally associated with snakes or boats or George but what their unique meaning is to *me*. Snakes often turn up in people's dreams, and sometimes they mean danger. Classically, they are associated with healing and also with sexuality. But they may turn up in *my* dream as a symbol of a happy childhood because I once had a pet carpet snake. Boats to you may mean leisure, fun and sailing, to me they may mean danger of drowning. George may be a great guy, and mayor of the city, but if he and I played chess together every Sunday when we were kids, it may be George as a chess player (and therefore my competitiveness, perhaps, or the way I plan the key moves in the game of my life) which is significant. He may even be a symbol of Sundays.

Working the dream

As you can see from Ann's account of her efforts to understand the dream, she is doing a lot of it with her intellect. She *"wonders," "has thoughts,"* tries to *"work it out,"* and *"comes to conclusions."* All *thinking* words. She gets there in the end. But sometimes it works best to get inside the dream again, at a *feeling* level.

One way to do that is to tell our dreams in the present tense. (Note how Ann switches to this, part way through the telling. She starts out in past tense but obviously gets more in touch with it as she tells it, so switches intuitively into the present tense.)

Then we can enter the dream and take the part of each element in turn. "I am a woman dressed as an Arab, wearing a turban. I am walking quickly down the street..."

By *being* the woman, and feeling her from the inside, Ann may soon begin to feel her own invincibility. And more of the woman's story may emerge.

If Ann had 'become' the kitten, and told the dream again but this time from the kitten's point of view, she may possibly not have had to wonder so long about its meaning. ("I am a kitten or a young cat, and right now I feel ...")

It is not just the live elements that we can become. One of the most vivid examples of this in my own dream life occurred way back when I had just graduated as a social worker and was excited about starting my first professional job. The night before I was to begin the new job, I dreamed of riding my bicycle happily down a path and noticing that the cement was not yet fully dry. It was only when I became the cement path and heard myself saying to the person on the bicycle "You can't ride on me yet. I'M NOT QUITE READY!" that I got in touch with the fear that underlay my confidence as a newly-minted social worker taking on a responsible job.

Ann latched on beautifully to this way of working with dreams and as she continued to work with this one she found more treasures in it. Becoming the city, she exclaimed *"It is pulsing with life. It is my body!"* and when she became the alleyway she immediately knew it represented her mind. But becoming the woman with the turban taught her even more about herself, especially when, to her surprise, she discovered that this woman had, *"a twin sister who vacillates, is weak & vulnerable, peevish at times and in general has many of the opposite qualities of her twin, she just didn't feature in the dream!"* At this point, she was already moving, intuitively, into the next process that I want to talk about, which is the one Carl Jung called Active Imagination.

Extending the dreamwork

Active Imagination is when we get into the dream elements and *carry the story forward*. We move beyond the events of the dream and bring our imagination to bear on what might happen next. It is as though the dream has given us the plot and some of the characters and written the first chapter and then handed over to us to keep telling the story.

You might say "But then it's just imagination." True. However, the storehouse from which our imaginations select their ingredients is the storehouse of our own minds. From an infinite variety of possibilities, we choose only certain ingredients. What motivates the choice? The unconscious mind, usually. It is our unconscious which throws up the raw material of imagination, just as it throws up the raw material of dreams. So Active Imagination, like the dream itself, can be full of fascinating information about what is really going on in our own, mysterious depths.

We spoke earlier about the Shadow: the unacknowledged, unlived aspects of ourselves. I said that in dreams the Shadow will often be represented by a dark figure or someone the dreamer can't quite see. There is no clear evidence of Ann's Shadow in this dream itself but when she announces: "I suspect the woman will have a twin sister who vacillates, is weak and vulnerable, peevish at times and in general has many of the opposite qualities of her twin, she just didn't feature in the dream!" this tells me Ann is already aware of—and fully owning—her Shadow, the flip side of the Persona that she presents to the world.

In dream groups, when a dream has been fully explored by the dreamer, other people are invited to add their feelings and impressions about it. Sometimes, that process can yield even more riches. It is only after all that has been completed that we might turn to dictionaries of symbols, just to see if there are further clues there. Since we are all connected, at a deep level, there are some symbols which resonate in the same way with everyone, and occasionally it helps to recall these universal meanings. But apart from that, please stay well away from books and articles which purport to decode your dreams. Your dreams are your own wonderful, meaningful creations, and the keys to the code are right there, within you. We should never consult decoders before we have done our own dreamwork.

Grounding the dreamwork

The final stage of working on a dream—the importance of which was brought home to me by the Jungian writer, Robert Johnson[6]—is to ground it in reality.

Our dreams are valuable entities. They are teachers, mirrors, guides. So it is only right that we should honor them by listening to them and taking them seriously. Making some action, whether practical or symbolic, to connect the message of the dream with our everyday, waking life, is a way of showing respect and gratitude to our dreaming selves. Secondly, it reinforces the teaching message of the dream by making it more real. Thirdly, it invites new directions in our personal growth process.

There are many ways in which Ann could ground this dream in the reality of her waking life. She could scoop up a little sand, and/or find a picture of the desert, and place these on her altar, if she has one. She could buy a little china kitten and put it on her bedside table. She could make up a name for her Arab self and write a poem to her. She could buy or make herself a pair of baggy trousers or obtain a recording of Middle Eastern music, dress up as an Arab and dance. She could get some essential oil which reminds her of the feeling of the dream. She could even go all the way and enroll for belly dancing classes! There are dozens of ways she could ground that dream in her everyday reality. That way it can continue to teach her, for it will now be woven right into the fabric of her life. She is already 'more' than she was before. This is individuation.

PART III

A CHANGE OF CONSCIOUSNESS

10

Your Transpersonal Self

If I have a physical problem, I need my health practitioner to see me not just as an example of a medical condition but holistically, i.e. as a whole person with a lifestyle, a set of relationships, a home, a belief system and so on, because any or all of these factors may be relevant to my healing. A therapist concerned with personal growth needs to have the kind of holistic approach that sees individuals in terms not only of their connection to the world they can see, hear, touch and feel but also their connection to everything seen and unseen, known and unknown. Your whole self includes not only your body, your feelings and emotions but also your spiritual life, the 'vibes' you emit and your consciousness of the unseen matrix in which you—and all of us—are embedded. We call this the transpersonal self.

The quantum universe

Sir Isaac Newton developed the concept of gravity after noticing that apples always fall downwards. But there actually is no universal 'up' or 'down;' an apple falling off a tree in Australia and one falling off a tree in England move in opposite directions. Everything is relative. If you toss a tennis ball in the air while you are inside a train carriage it will come down in the same place, even if the train is going at 120 mph. There is really no such thing as time. There is no such thing as a straight line (only the *concept* of a straight line). The chair you are sitting on is not really solid at all because when you break down solid matter into its constituent parts you end up with elementary particles that are so unstable they appear to blink in and out of existence, sometimes appearing as particles and sometimes as waves. If you take two spinning particles that were once joined and send them in different directions but then change the direction of spin on one of them, the other will change direction to match, even though there is no longer any apparent connection between them.

Although Newtonian physics, with its ideas of up and down and speed and time and all of that, is a perfectly adequate science for our everyday lives, the truth is that we live in a quantum world. It is a much weirder world than the good old reliable Newtonian one and it is a world that even the most knowledgeable physicists still know very little about, yet it is our own world, the one we breathe in and move about in and whose ways we think we understand.

In fact, all we can really understand is that which we can perceive with our senses. Just as a cat or a dog can hear high frequency sounds that are inaudible to the human ear, there are many, many other things around us that are completely inaccessible to us because of the limitations of our sensory apparatus. Even when we use sophisticated machines to extend our perception, such as radio telescopes, the interpretation of our results can only be done by means of that same sensory apparatus and the understanding of them can only be done by our human minds. The finite, human mind cannot totally grasp infinity, yet the universe might well be infinite and plural. There are energies and forces we don't normally perceive with our senses, but they are none the less real. We can often feel their effects, just as we are aware of the effects of magnets even though magnetism is an invisible force. Some, we can easily learn to discern. The Eastern concept of 'chi' is a good example. Anyone who has studied one of the martial arts will be aware of this invisible energy and will have learned how to feel it, use it and work with it. When we learn to channel universal energy, our strength, stamina and creativity are all hugely increased and we can help others deal with their problems without it dragging us down.

Worlds unseen

There are almost certainly dimensions of existence that inter-penetrate our own even though we are normally unaware of them and occasionally there may be a bleed through and someone has an experience that is labeled 'paranormal' or 'supernatural.' In fact, as various polls have shown, at least half of us have had some sort of experience like that, however fleeting. Even if we have not, a majority of us seem to believe such experiences to be possible. So in most people there is obviously an interest in the dimensions of ourselves and our universe that are way beyond the everyday, familiar ones. Learning about these things, reading about the mysteries science has been unraveling and pondering on all the mysteries as yet unraveled, is something lots of us find fascinating. Not only does it fascinate us but it broadens our awareness and understanding of our place in the greater scheme of things, just as the realization that the world was round and not flat did for our ancestors.

Time

Of all the illusions modern physics has busted, probably the hardest to deal with is time. We are programmed to see life sequentially—like watching a movie—whereas imagining the same movie wound in its canister and lying on the table might in fact be a more accurate way of understanding it. The key to experiencing this sort of timeless awareness is to remain as much as possible in the 'now' of the present moment, and there are many good books and teachers to help us learn how to do this. Also, a very useful self-therapy technique is to ask your OS to notice not only when your mind moves away from the 'now' but where it goes when it does so.[7]

A sense of oneness

The most amazing realization that has yet to penetrate the awareness of more than a small percentage of the human population is Gaia Theory: the idea, first proposed by scientists Lovelock and Margulis, that the planet itself is able to self-regulate exactly as though it is one huge, living organism. In all likelihood, that is precisely what it is.

In which case, we are not isolated individuals at all but cells in the body of a larger being.

When you think of it this way, the experiences that so many people have, especially in meditation, of feeling at one with everyone and everything, make perfect sense. We *are* all one. We are all connected in the same way that individual leaves on a tree, although each one is different, are all connected by being part of the tree. That collective unconscious that I compared to the deepest layers of couch grass in the garden, is like the leaf's awareness of the tree roots.

If we could all not only become fully aware of our oneness with all the rest of life on Earth but *live out of* that awareness, think how much easier it would be to co-exist peacefully, co-operatively and sustainably. Right there is one good reason for becoming aware of your transpersonal self.

It is also an awareness that can help to allay fear, for example the fear of death. Leaves shrivel and fall to the ground and become compost and from compost comes new life. Every single thing that exists here on Earth (with the exception of a few meteorites and some dust from space) has been here since the world began and will continue to be here as long as the planet exists. All that happens is a constant shape-shifting and recycling.

It is an awareness that can give you a respite from

burnout. When you look at everything from a transpersonal perspective it is like looking at the Earth from space. Small things that loomed large when you were on the ground are suddenly reduced in size and importance. If you were fretting about not having time to mow the lawn, try going to the Internet and looking your house up on Google Earth. Then keep clicking on the little minus sign and your lawn will soon disappear altogether!

The secret truth of relationship

One of the most useful reasons for developing an awareness of your transpersonal self is that it helps you to understand the deepest underlying dynamics of your interactions with other people. Irrespective of what we say and do and pretend, the *real* message of any interaction between two or more living organisms is transmitted on an energy level that most of the time we are only dimly aware of. The words and actions themselves are just the packaging it comes in. So if you think of someone lovingly, your love reaches them at some level, whether they are consciously aware of it or not. And if you and they exchange loving thoughts, then whether that is via email or via an in-person hug makes no difference. By the same token, when people give each other meaningless air kisses and there is no loving energy being transmitted, they may as well not bother. When you dislike a person and think critical thoughts about them, even if you paste a smile on your face as you shake hands with them you will not really be fooling them, even though they may be choosing to ignore the messages coming from that deeper part of their psyche that knows the truth. If you are sexually aroused by someone and allow yourself to imagine having sex with them, there is a movement of energy that the other person will feel, even if only at a very subtle level. Even young children are susceptible to this, which is why we teach them to be aware of any discomfort around certain people.

The same applies to feelings of rage and potential violence. If someone is angry with us we usually know it, even if they are saying nothing. Other animals, too, can pick up our vibes and read our intentions.

We might think we can hide from each other but we really cannot, and anybody who really cares enough to see through our masks can do so anyway. We only keep wearing them because most of the time we manage to kid ourselves that they work and we can go on kidding ourselves that they work because everybody colludes in pretending that they do.

The dropping of masks in favor of personal authenticity is thus a high-level step in self-therapy.

And finally…

I hope the time you spend learning and practicing self-therapy helps you to heal, to know and understand yourself better, to learn and to grow. But just a word of warning: the other two important pieces of graffiti in Delphi said 'μηδεν ἀγαν' which means 'Nothing in excess' and Ἐγγύα πάρα δ'ἄτη,' usually translated as, 'Make a pledge and mischief is nigh.' So please remember to (a) relax, kick back and have fun as well and (b) not to be too hard on yourself if you sometimes fall back into old ways of thinking and behaving. Changing patterns is not always easy.

Bearing that in mind, please remember to be kind and gentle towards others around you who are still playing their games and presumably not trying to know themselves better. We are all working on different tasks, at different speeds and in different ways. None of us can know what lessons another person's soul has designed for them. Compassion rules, OK?

Remember that every relationship we have with other

people in our lives is a mirror that enables us to see ourselves more clearly. So in fact everyone you meet is your teacher. Remember, too, that ultimately you have nothing to offer anyone except the quality of your presence.

I wish you a wonderful and fascinating journey.

Notes

1. Berne and his successors outlined many other concepts useful for self-understanding and I encourage you to explore them. Google 'Transactional Analysis' to find a host of useful links.
2. Hillman, J. *The Soul's Code: In search of character and calling* Grand Central Publishing (1997)
3. Various questionnaires have been developed to determine people's Myers-Briggs type. The official test needs to be administered by a qualified professional. There are free tests online but not all are reliable. The one I tried at http://www.humanmetrics.com/cgi-win/jtypes 2.asp proved accurate for me.
   Myers, I.B, and Myers, P.B. *Gifts Differing: Understanding Personality Type*
   Davies-Black Publishing (1980,1995) remains the best book for understanding the 16 types.
4. Plotkin, B. *Nature and the Human Soul: Cultivating Wholeness and Community in a Fragmented World* New World Library (2007)
5. The original classic for tuning into the body's messages, first published in 1951 and later republished with a new introduction:
   Perls, F.S., Hefferline, R. & Goodman, P. *Gestalt Therapy: Excitement and Growth in the Human Personality* The Gestalt Journal Press (1977)
6. Johnson, R. *Inner Work: Using Dreams and Active Imagination for Personal Growth* Harper & Row (1989)
7. Richard Moss writes eloquently about this technique in this beautiful book which I highly recommend: Moss, R. *The Mandala of Being: Discovering the Power of Awareness* New World Library (2007)

About the Author

Marian Van Eyk McCain BSW (Melbourne), MA, East-West Psychology (C.I.I.S. San Francisco) is a retired transpersonal psychotherapist and health educator, now enjoying her incarnation as a freelance writer on a range of subjects, including psychology, women's health, aging, wellness, simplicity, green spirituality, environmental issues, organic growing and alternative technology.

She is the author of eight books (details at **www.marian vaneykmccain.com**), co-editor of the magazine 'GreenSpirit' and also a blogger, columnist and book reviewer. A lover of all things green, she lives, very simply, in rural Devon with her soulmate and partner, Sky McCain. She welcomes visits to her books website (above) and to her primary website at **www.elderwoman.org**

**PSYCHE
BOOKS**

The study of the mind: interactions, behaviours, functions.
Developing and learning our understanding of self. Psyche
Books cover all aspects of psychology and matters relating to
the head.